TEAM SPIRIT®

SMART BOOKS FOR YOUNG FANS

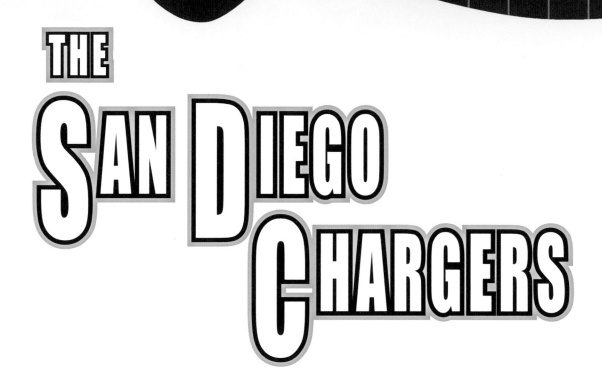

THE SAN DIEGO CHARGERS

BY
MARK STEWART

NORWOOD HOUSE PRESS

CHICAGO, ILLINOIS

Norwood House Press
P.O. Box 316598
Chicago, Illinois 60631

For information regarding Norwood House Press, please visit our website at:
www.norwoodhousepress.com or call 866-565-2900.

All photos courtesy of Getty Images except the following:
Icon SMI (4), Xerographics, Inc. (6),
Black Book Partners (7, 8, 9, 10, 11, 14, 25, 27, 28, 35 top right, 36, 37, 41, 43 left, 45),
Topps, Inc. (15, 19, 23, 38, 42 top & bottom left, 43 top & bottom right),
Fleer Corp. (20, 34 left), San Diego Chargers/NFL (21, 22, 34 right),
Author's Collection (33), Matt Richman (48).
Cover Photo: Icon SMI

The memorabilia and artifacts pictured in this book are presented for educational and informational purposes,
and come from the collection of the author.

Editor: Mike Kennedy
Designer: Ron Jaffe
Project Management: Black Book Partners, LLC.
Special thanks to Topps, Inc.

Library of Congress Cataloging-in-Publication Data

Stewart, Mark, 1960-
  The San Diego Chargers / by Mark Stewart. -- Rev. ed.
    p. cm. -- (Team spirit)
  Includes bibliographical references and index.
  Summary: "A revised Team Spirit Football edition featuring the San Diego
Chargers that chronicles the history and accomplishments of the team.
Includes access to the Team Spirit website which provides additional
information and photos"--Provided by publisher.
  ISBN 978-1-59953-537-1 (library edition : alk. paper) -- ISBN
978-1-60357-479-2 (ebook)
  1. San Diego Chargers (Football team)--History--Juvenile literature. I.
Title.
  GV956.S29S84 2012
  796.332'6409794985--dc23

                                                    2012015467

Manufactured in the United States of America in North Mankato, Minnesota.
205N—082012

COVER PHOTO: The Chargers celebrate a good defensive play during the 2011 season.

Table of Contents

ABOUT OUR GLOSSARY

In this book, there may be several words that you are reading for the first time. Some are sports words, some are new vocabulary words, and some are familiar words that are used in an unusual way. All of these words are defined on page 46. Throughout the book, sports words appear in **bold type**. Regular vocabulary words appear in ***bold italic type***.

Meet the Chargers

N othing in nature strikes faster or with more power than a bolt of lightning. On any given Sunday, the same could be said of the San Diego Chargers. For more than 50 seasons, the Chargers have specialized in scoring spectacular touchdowns and making bone-jarring tackles.

Year after year, the Chargers find players who combine tremendous talent and leadership—plus a special gift for doing things that make the fans jump out of their seats. However, the team is more than a collection of a few stars. When everyone does their job and every play is run to perfection, San Diego is simply unstoppable.

This book tells the story of the Chargers. There's an old saying that lightning never strikes twice. Don't tell that to football fans in San Diego. Every time they settle into their seats for a game, they are expecting nothing less than a bolt from the blue.

On any given Sunday, the Chargers are likely to amaze fans with exciting plays. Sometimes, they even amaze themselves!

Glory Days

The 1960s were a lot of fun for football fans. For the first time, people tuned in by the millions to watch games on television. Exciting new college stars graduated to the *professional* game in huge numbers each year. There was actually enough talent for two leagues. In 1960, the **American Football League (AFL)** began play alongside the older **National Football League (NFL)**. The Chargers were one of two AFL teams in California—the Oakland Raiders were the other. The Chargers played their first year in Los Angeles. In 1961, they moved south to San Diego.

The Chargers had the AFL's best coaching staff. Sid Gillman, Al Davis, and Chuck Noll were all football geniuses. They turned a group of unknown players into winners. From 1960 to 1965, the Chargers reached the **AFL Championship Game** five times. Quarterbacks Jack Kemp,

Tobin Rote, and John Hadl were the team leaders. They had two swift and powerful runners, Paul Lowe and Keith Lincoln. Their best receiver was Lance Alworth. He joined the Chargers in 1962 and became the AFL's most exciting player. San Diego won its one and only league championship in 1963.

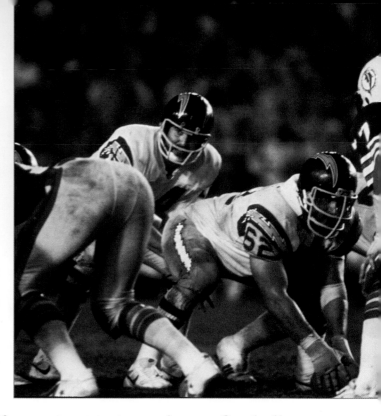

The NFL and AFL joined forces in 1970, and pro football became more popular than ever. Now part of the NFL's **American Football Conference (AFC)**, the Chargers spent many years trying to rebuild the team. San Diego used the same recipe for success as it had in the 1960s—a quick-striking offense and a good defense. From 1978 to 1981, the Chargers were the most thrilling team in the NFL. Their leader was a tough, strong-armed quarterback named Dan Fouts. He threw for more than 4,000 yards three seasons in a row. His favorite targets were Charlie Joiner, Kellen Winslow, John Jefferson, and Wes Chandler. Pass-rushers Louie Kelcher and Fred Dean starred on defense.

LEFT: Lance Alworth was the AFL's top receiver.
ABOVE: Dan Fouts keeps a close eye on the defense.

The Chargers reached the **Super Bowl** for the first time in 1994. Defensive stars Junior Seau and Leslie O'Neal led the team. Seau was a fierce tackler who played the entire year with a painful shoulder injury. O'Neal loved to **sack** the quarterback. San Diego's quarterback was Stan Humphries. He was not a superstar, but he always seemed to make big plays to win the close games. Humphries got plenty of help from Natrone Means, who ran for 1,350 yards and 12 touchdowns. Tony Martin was the team's top receiver.

In the years that followed, the Chargers struggled to find the right combination of stars again. They went through many up-and-down seasons. In 2000, San Diego lost 15 of its 16 games.

The team rebuilt around LaDainian Tomlinson, a talented halfback who ran with speed and power. He burst through holes

LEFT: LaDainian Tomlinson gained over 1,000 yards eight seasons in a row.
ABOVE: Junior Seau gets ready to make a defensive stop.

opened by a good offensive line that included Chris Dielman, Marcus McNeill, and Nick Hardwick. They also protected a pair of **Pro Bowl** quarterbacks, first Drew Brees and then Philip Rivers.

Antonio Gates also developed into a dangerous weapon. The big tight end reminded some fans of Winslow. Gates was big and strong, and he could also outrun most defenders who tried to cover him. In 2004, Gates's second season, the Chargers returned to the top of the **AFC West**. Two years later, they finished with the best record in the NFL.

Defense was a big part of San Diego's success in the first *decade* of the 21st century. Shawne Merriman, Shaun Phillips, Luis Castillo, and Jamal Williams kept the heat on opposing quarterbacks. Antonio Cromartie, Quentin Jammer, and Eric Weddle made passing against the Chargers very difficult.

In 2007, San Diego returned to the **AFC Championship Game** for the first time in 13 years. Tomlinson had become the NFL's most feared runner, and Rivers was being praised for his toughness and *poise*. In 2009, Rivers led the Chargers on another great run. After beginning the year 2–3, San Diego "ran the table" and won all 11 of its remaining games. Unfortunately, the Chargers fell short of the Super Bowl again.

In 2010, San Diego began a plan to remake the team. After Tomlinson left the Chargers, they gave a lot of responsibility to younger players, such as Darren Sproles, Ryan Mathews, Mike Tolbert, and Antoine Cason. At the end of the year, the Chargers amazed the experts by having the best offense and best defense in the league.

San Diego fans have begun rooting for a whole new *generation* of players. As these young stars continue to grow, Sunday will always be a fun day in San Diego.

LEFT: Antonio Gates heads up the field after a catch.   **ABOVE**: Yeah! Philip Rivers celebrates a touchdown against the Tampa Bay Buccaneers.

Home Turf

After their one season in Los Angeles in 1960, the Chargers moved to San Diego. The team's first home there was Balboa Stadium. It was a cozy park set on a hill above downtown San Diego. In 1967, the team moved into its current home, San Diego Stadium. It has gone by other names over the years, including Jack Murphy Stadium, which was named in honor of a famous sportswriter. The Chargers shared the stadium with the Padres baseball team for more than three decades.

San Diego's stadium is one of the oldest in the NFL. It has been improved several times. Fans like it because every seat has a good view of the field. One day soon, the Chargers hope to play in a modern stadium. San Diego fans hope so, too.

BY THE NUMBERS

- The Chargers' stadium has 71,500 seats.
- Improvements to the stadium have cost nearly $90 million.
- The entire stadium site sits on 166 acres of land.

Fans enjoy another warm, cloudless day at a Chargers game.

Dressed for Success

A charger is the name for a horse used in battle by *medieval* knights. However, San Diego's *logo* is a lightning bolt. It has been on the team's helmets and uniforms every year since 1960. The Chargers also used a horse head and shield in their logo during the 1960s.

San Diego's colors are blue, gold, and white. In their first 14 seasons, the Chargers used light blue. In the 1970s, they switched to a darker shade of blue, and then changed to an even darker shade beginning in 1988. The Chargers still wear their old light-blue uniforms on special occasions.

Fans around the NFL agree that the Chargers have one of the best uniforms in the league. They love the lightning bolt, especially as it now appears on the team's helmet. In 2007, San Diego switched to a white helmet with a gold and blue bolt.

EARL FAISON
SAN DIEGO CHARGERS   DEF. END

LEFT: Antoine Cason heads for the end zone in San Diego's road uniform.
ABOVE: Earl Faison poses in the team's uniform from the early 1960s.

We Won!

Football fans love a winner. The Chargers made their fans very happy by winning the AFL's **Western Division** in each of their first two seasons. Unfortunately, they lost to the Houston Oilers for the league title both times.

In 1962, San Diego had a down year and did not make the **playoffs**. Coach Sid Gillman decided his team needed to get tougher. In the summer of 1963, he sent his players to an abandoned ranch called Rough Acres. Gillman put them through the hardest workouts of their lives. The results spoke for themselves.

The Chargers rolled from the first week of the 1963 season.

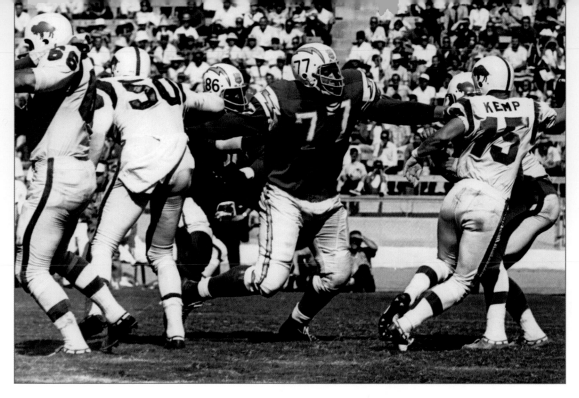

They went 11–3 and finished first in their division. Paul Lowe led the team with 1,010 rushing yards. Keith Lincoln averaged 6.5 yards every time he carried the ball. Lance Alworth caught 61 passes and scored 11 touchdowns. Tobin Rote, a 35-year-old who had played in Canada the year before, was the AFL's top-rated quarterback.

The San Diego defense was just as dangerous. Earl Faison and Ernie Ladd put pressure on opposing quarterbacks and forced them into making bad throws. Dick Harris and Chuck Allen led a great **secondary**. The Chargers intercepted 29 passes in 14 games.

San Diego's main competition came from the Oakland Raiders. Their coach was Al Davis. He had started his career with the Chargers,

LEFT: Paul Lowe strikes a pose during training camp.
ABOVE: Ernie Ladd creates problems for the Buffalo Bills.

so he knew the team very well. Oakland beat San Diego twice during the regular season, but the Chargers still managed to finish in front of the Raiders.

The Chargers faced the Boston Patriots in the AFL Championship Game. Boston had a hard-hitting defense. On this day, however, the Chargers ruled. On San Diego's second play, Lincoln ran right up the middle for a 56-yard gain. Moments later, Rote snuck into the end zone for the game's first touchdown. The next time San Diego had the ball, Lincoln ran for a 67-yard score. Later in the first quarter, Lowe sprinted for a 58-yard touchdown. The score was 21–7 after just 15 minutes.

The Patriots could do nothing to stop the Chargers. Alworth caught a 48-yard pass in the third quarter to make the score 38–10. In the fourth quarter, young John Hadl replaced Rote. He threw a 25-yard touchdown pass to Lincoln and also ran for a touchdown.

The San Diego defense, meanwhile, stopped the Patriots cold. The Chargers did not allow a point in the second half. They held Boston to just 261 yards. San Diego won 51–10 to claim the AFL title.

The star of stars was Lincoln.

KEITH LINCOLN
SAN DIEGO CHARGERS   FULLBACK

He scored three times and finished the day with 206 rushing yards. He had another 123 yards receiving. Lincoln also threw a pass for 20 yards. Most experts agree that it was the greatest performance in the 10-year history of the AFL.

"I can still see Keith Lincoln," said Larry Eisenhauer of the Patriots many years later. "Every time he touched the ball, he gained 20 yards. He caught passes for touchdowns. He even completed a pass."

LEFT: Lance Alworth runs to daylight against the Boston Patriots.
ABOVE: Keith Lincoln had plenty to smile about after the 1963 AFL title game.

Go-To Guys

To be a true star in the NFL, you need more than fast feet and a big body. You have to be a "go-to guy"—someone the coach wants on the field at the end of a big game. Chargers fans have had a lot to cheer about over the years, including these great stars …

THE PIONEERS

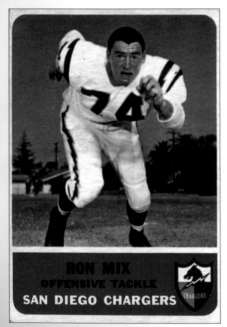

RON MIX
OFFENSIVE TACKLE
SAN DIEGO CHARGERS

RON MIX   Offensive Lineman

- BORN: 3/10/1938
- PLAYED FOR TEAM: 1960 TO 1969

Ron Mix teamed up with Ernie Wright to form the best blocking duo in the AFL. Mix was smart, fast, and extremely strong. He was penalized for holding only twice in his 10 seasons with the Chargers.

EARL FAISON   Defensive Lineman

- BORN: 1/31/1939
- PLAYED FOR TEAM: 1961 TO 1966

Earl Faison was one of the AFL's best pass-rushers in the early 1960s. In his first season, he was voted Rookie of the Year. He was named **All-AFL** in each of his five years in San Diego.

LANCE ALWORTH Receiver

- BORN: 8/3/1940 • PLAYED FOR TEAM: 1962 TO 1970

Lance Alworth was nicknamed "Bambi" because of his speed and leaping ability. He was voted All-AFL seven seasons in a row. Alworth was also the first player from the AFL to be elected to the **Hall of Fame**.

WALT SWEENEY Offensive Lineman

- BORN: 4/18/1941 • PLAYED FOR TEAM: 1963 TO 1973

Walt Sweeney was San Diego's first pick in the 1963 AFL **draft**. He was a powerful blocker who helped Paul Lowe and Keith Lincoln run for nearly 2,000 yards that season. Sweeney made the Pro Bowl nine times.

DAN FOUTS Quarterback

- BORN: 6/10/1951 • PLAYED FOR TEAM: 1973 TO 1987

Dan Fouts was one of the best passers in football history. He was a great leader who always stood his ground. Fouts shared honors as the **Most Valuable Player (MVP)** in the 1983 Pro Bowl and guided the Chargers to the AFC Championship Game twice.

CHARLIE JOINER Receiver

- BORN: 10/14/1947 • PLAYED FOR TEAM: 1976 TO 1986

Charlie Joiner was a very clever receiver. He could read defenses better than most coaches and always knew how to find a hole between defenders. Joiner caught nearly 600 passes and scored 47 touchdowns for the Chargers.

LEFT: Ron Mix
RIGHT: Charlie Joiner

KELLEN WINSLOW   Tight End

• BORN: 11/5/1957   • PLAYED FOR TEAM: 1979 TO 1987

Kellen Winslow was the perfect tight end. He was a good blocker, but his greatest talent was as a receiver. Winslow led the AFC in catches three years in a row and once caught five touchdown passes in a game.

LESLIE O'NEAL   Defensive Lineman

• BORN: 5/7/1964   • PLAYED FOR TEAM: 1986 TO 1995

Leslie O'Neal was so fast that opponents weren't sure how to block him. He was at his best rushing the passer. O'Neal had at least 10 sacks in seven seasons and was voted **All-Pro** five times.

JUNIOR SEAU   Linebacker

• BORN: 1/19/1969   • DIED: 5/2/2012   • PLAYED FOR TEAM: 1990 TO 2002

Junior Seau had an amazing combination of brains and brute strength. He seemed to know where every play was headed and usually made the tackle. With the Chargers, Seau proved he was one of the NFL's greatest leaders.

LaDAINIAN TOMLINSON   Running Back

• BORN: 6/23/1979   • PLAYED FOR TEAM: 2001 TO 2009

From his first game with the Chargers, LaDainian Tomlinson showed he could do it all. In 2003, he became the first player to rush for 1,000 yards and catch 100 passes in the same season. Three years later, Tomlinson set an NFL record with 31 touchdowns in one season.

ANTONIO GATES — Tight End

• BORN: 6/18/1980   • FIRST YEAR WITH TEAM: 2003

Antonio Gates was a basketball star in college, which is why no NFL team drafted him. When he tried out for the Chargers, they realized he had the *potential* to be a great tight end. Gates averaged 13 yards per reception in his first nine seasons and was voted All-Pro three times.

PHILIP RIVERS — Quarterback

• BORN: 12/8/1981   • FIRST YEAR WITH TEAM: 2004

Philip Rivers became the Chargers' starting quarterback when he was 24. He quickly showed the talent and leadership of a *veteran*. In 2007, Rivers played through the pain of a badly injured leg and led the Chargers to the AFC Championship Game. In 2010, he topped the NFL with 4,710 passing yards.

ERIC WEDDLE — Defensive Back

• BORN: 1/4/1985   • FIRST YEAR WITH TEAM: 2007

The Chargers traded three players just so they could draft Eric Weddle. He was worth the high price. Weddle used his speed and toughness to become an All-Pro safety. In 2011, he led the Chargers with seven **interceptions**.

LEFT: Kellen Winslow
RIGHT: Eric Weddle

Calling the Shots

The Chargers had a big advantage in their early years. Their coach was Sid Gillman. He changed the way the game was played. Gillman believed that football was not a contest of strength, but rather a test of speed and skill. He was the first coach who "stretched" the field by having his team throw long passes. When defenses tried to stop the pass, San Diego's runners found more openings.

Two of Gillman's assistants also became famous coaches. Al Davis worked with the team's receivers for three years before he became the coach (and later owner) of the Oakland Raiders. Chuck Noll taught defenders new moves to fend off blockers and rush the quarterback. Noll later coached the Pittsburgh Steelers to four Super Bowl wins.

Another San Diego coach who believed in winning with offense was Don Coryell. He led the team from 1978 to 1986. Under Coryell, San Diego had the NFL's best passing attack. Fans called it "Air Coryell."

Bobby Ross took San Diego to its first Super Bowl. He was a dedicated coach who expected his players to work just as hard as he did. Ross made the Chargers believe in themselves, and the team became one of the best in the NFL.

In recent years, the Chargers have had other excellent coaches, including Marty Schottenheimer and Norv Turner. Schottenheimer was all about details. He taught his players to do all the little things that help win games. Turner led the team to the 2007 AFC Championship Game in his first season.

One Great Day

At the beginning of the 1994 season, many fans thought the Chargers might finish in last place. San Diego surprised everyone by winning one close game after another. The team ended up with 11 wins and captured the AFC West crown. In the playoffs, the Chargers reached the AFC Championship Game, where they faced the Pittsburgh Steelers.

More than 60,000 fans jammed into Pittsburgh's Three Rivers Stadium for the contest. The Chargers felt confident. Junior Seau reminded his teammates that they had surprised a lot of teams already, including the Steelers. The Chargers had beaten them a few weeks earlier. "We've been *underdogs* all the way through the season," Seau said.

The game started badly for the Chargers. Pittsburgh led 10–3 at halftime and added a **field goal** in the third quarter. Stan Humphries gave San Diego a much-needed lift. On a pass play, he spotted

Stan Humphries fires a pass against the Pittsburgh Steelers.

Alfred Pupunu in the clear down the field and hit him in stride with a perfect strike. The big tight end ran into the end zone for a 43-yard touchdown.

With less than six minutes left in the game, Humphries fired another 43-yard touchdown pass, this time to Tony Martin. The Chargers went ahead 17–13. The Steelers got the ball back and marched deep into San Diego territory. On fourth down, linebacker Dennis Gibson knocked a pass out of the air that would have put Pittsburgh ahead. The Chargers were AFC champions for the first time in team history!

"We just kept fighting and coming back," a tired Humphries said after the game. "Like we did all year."

Legend Has It

Who was the most dangerous Charger?

LEGEND HAS IT that Darren Sproles was. In a 2008 game, Sproles had over 50 rushing yards, 50 receiving yards, and 100 yards in kick returns. He was just the second player in NFL history to accomplish this feat. Later in the season, Sproles had 328 all-purpose yards in a *dramatic* win during the playoffs. Only two players in league history had ever gained more yards in a **postseason** game.

: Darren Sproles leaves a tackler clutching at air.

LEGEND HAS IT that it was Philip Rivers. Rivers worked as a counselor at Peyton Manning's Passing Academy one summer when he was in college. One of the other counselors was Peyton's brother Eli. On draft day in 2004, the Chargers traded Eli to the New York Giants for Rivers.

Were the 2010 Chargers the best team ever to *not* make the playoffs?

LEGEND HAS IT that they were. When the 2010 season started, only seven teams in history had finished with the NFL's top-rated offense and top-rated defense in the same year. The Chargers became the eighth. Unfortunately, mistakes early in the season led to several losses in September and October. As luck would have it, the Chargers fell short of the playoffs by one victory.

It Really Happened

The 1981 Chargers were a tough and talented team. No one symbolized those qualities better than Kellen Winslow. He led San Diego with 88 receptions for 1,075 yards and 10 touchdowns. Winslow was one of many offensive stars for San Diego. The team gained nearly 7,000 yards on the season and led the NFL with 478 points. The Chargers rode their high-flying offense to a 10–6 record and a spot in the playoffs. They faced the Miami Dolphins in the first round.

The game was tense, and Winslow was unstoppable. He caught 13 passes for 166 yards and a touchdown. He also helped open holes for Chuck Muncie, who rushed for 120 yards. San Diego trailed by seven points with time running out when Gary Johnson and Linden King forced a fumble by the Dolphins. The Chargers pounced on the loose ball.

With a chance to tie the score, Dan Fouts drove San Diego down the field. He threw a touchdown pass to James Brooks with less than a minute to play. The Dolphins came right back. On the last

An exhausted Kellen Winslow is helped off the field.

play of the fourth quarter, they tried a game-winning field goal. Winslow—who stood 6′ 5″—crashed between two blockers, leaped through the air, and tipped the ball. The game went into **overtime**.

The Chargers had the first chance to win, but Rolf Benirschke missed a field goal. He got another chance as time ticked away in the extra period. This time, his kick was perfect for a 41–38 victory.

The next day, many fans said it was the greatest game they ever saw. Fouts agreed. "Without a doubt, this was the most exciting game I've ever been involved with," he said. "This may have been the best-played game ever between two football teams in a playoff."

Team Spirit

The Chargers have always had a close relationship with their fans. The team is known for reaching out to the young people of Southern California. Every year, the Chargers give money to help youth sports programs. During the season, they honor a different high school football coach each week and make a donation to his school. At the end of the year, team owner Alex Spanos holds an All-Star Game for the top players in the city.

Chargers fans are very well organized. They chat on the Internet and meet before games. The weather is normally beautiful in San Diego, so fans love to throw fun tailgate parties before home games. Once inside the stadium, they usually keep an eye on the Charger Girls, the team's cheerleading squad. They have been voted the NFL's best on several occasions.

LEFT: San Diego fans are creative in the ways they support the team.
ABOVE: This button was sold at the Chargers' stadium in the 1960s.

Timeline

In this timeline, each Super Bowl is listed under the year it was played. Remember that the Super Bowl is held early in the year and is actually part of the previous season. For example, Super Bowl XLVI was played on February 5, 2012, but it was the championship of the 2011 NFL season.

1981
Dan Fouts throws for 4,802 yards and 33 touchdowns.

1963
The Chargers win the AFL championship.

1960
The Chargers play their first season, in Los Angeles.

1972
John Hadl is voted to the Pro Bowl for the fifth time.

1985
Lionel James leads the AFC with 86 catches.

Paul Maguire was a star for the team in 1960.

PAUL MAGUIRE
END

LOS ANGELES CHARGERS

Lionel "Little Train" James

Tony Martin led the 1995 Super Bowl team with 90 catches.

Vincent Jackson starred for the 2008 team.

1995
The Chargers play in Super Bowl XXIX.

2004
Antonio Gates sets a record for tight ends with 13 touchdowns.

2008
The Chargers reach the AFC Championship Game.

1992
Leslie O'Neal leads the AFC with 17 sacks.

2006
LaDainian Tomlinson scores 31 touchdowns.

2010
Shaun Phillips makes his first Pro Bowl.

Shaun Phillips

Fun Facts

GOING LONG

In a 2007 game, Antonio Cromartie set an NFL record when he returned a missed field goal 109 yards for a touchdown. It was the longest play in league history.

FINISH STRONG

The Chargers are known for their slow starts, but they are also famous for their fast finishes. From 2006 to 2009, the team tied a record by winning 18 games in a row in December.

A GOOD LADD

For many years, Ernie Ladd was the Chargers' team ping-pong champion. Although he stood 6′ 9″ and weighed 320 pounds, his long arms and quick reflexes made him unbeatable. After football, Ladd turned to another sport: pro wrestling.

ABOVE: Antonio Cromartie
RIGHT: Rolf Benirschke

JUST FOR KICKS

From 1977 to 1986, San Diego's star kicker was Rolf Benirschke. After his playing days, Benirschke hosted game shows, including *Wheel of Fortune*.

GAME CHANGERS

Today's NFL tight ends owe a lot to the Chargers. Coach Don Coryell and Kellen Winslow changed the position in the 1980s. Teams now look for players just like Winslow, who can outrun linebackers and are too big to be covered by defensive backs.

IN A LEAGUE OF HIS OWN

In 1999, *The Sporting News* made a list of the 100 greatest football players in history. Lance Alworth was rated higher than any player who spent more than one season in the AFL.

I LOVE L.A.

When kicker Ben Agajanian joined the Chargers in 1960, he became the only player to suit up for all three pro teams in Los Angeles. During his career, Agajanian played for the Rams, Chargers, and a third club called the Dons.

Talking Football

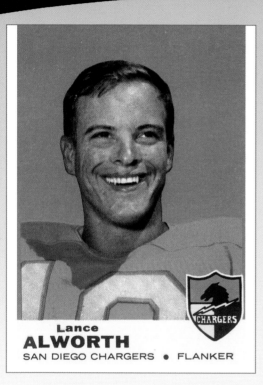

Lance
ALWORTH
SAN DIEGO CHARGERS • FLANKER

"It's really fun to see the guys asking for your autograph because it's been forty-some odd years since I played."
▶ *Lance Alworth, on his visits to San Diego practices*

"Sid just left a huge thumbprint on the game of football. The talk of 'stretching the field' that you hear today was exactly what he was saying back then."
▶ *Keith Lincoln, on Sid Gillman*

"There's no way I would have had the success I had, if I hadn't been traded to San Diego. That's when my career took off."
▶ *Charlie Joiner, on his years with the Chargers*

"I know I can be the difference in us winning and losing a game."
▶ *Eric Weddle, on why he gives 100 percent on every play*

"It was an attitude of fearlessness and aggressiveness and of fun. He was not afraid to try new things."

► **Dan Fouts,** *on what made Don Coryell a great coach*

"I like to run up the middle and wear defenses down. It's more exciting in between the tackles."

► **LaDainian Tomlinson,** *on why he wasn't afraid to attack the heart of the defense*

"I'm out there having as good a time as I did in the backyard since I was five years old."

► **Philip Rivers,** *on his love of football*

LEFT: Lance Alworth
ABOVE: Don Coryell and Dan Fouts

Great Debates

People who root for the Chargers love to compare their favorite moments, teams, and players. Some debates have been going on for years! How would you settle these classic football arguments?

The 1994 Chargers would have defeated the 1963 Chargers ...

... because they had a "big play" team. Junior Seau, Leslie O'Neal (   ), Chris Mims, Shawn Lee, and Darrien Gordon made game-changing plays on defense. Natrone Means ran like a human bowling ball, while Stan Humphries could throw to five different receivers. Even kicker John Carney had a great season. He missed only four field goals all year.

Not a chance! The 1963 Chargers would win ...

... because they were masters at stretching the field. Tobin Rote and Lance Alworth could connect for a touchdown at any time. Paul Lowe and Keith Lincoln were great at breaking tackles for big gains. All four were All-AFL that season. Meanwhile, everyone forgets that the Chargers didn't just have the league's top offense in 1963. They also allowed the fewest points in the AFL.

Philip Rivers was San Diego's greatest quarterback ...

... because the numbers say so. Heading into 2012, Rivers (   ) had a **quarterback rating** of 95.9 for his career. No Charger has ever been better than that. In fact, only two other quarterbacks in pro football history have been rated higher. In 2008, Rivers led the NFL with 34 touchdown passes. Two years later, he threw for more than 4,700 yards—the most in the league.

Not even close. Dan Fouts wins this battle ...

... because he made playing quarterback look so easy. Fouts had a great arm and amazing instincts. His receivers darted all over the field, and Fouts could whip the ball to them wherever they were. In 1980, he became the first quarterback to throw for 4,700 yards in a season. In 1981, he threw for over 4,800 yards.

For the Record

The great Chargers teams and players have left their marks on the record books. These are the "best of the best" ...

CHARGERS AWARD WINNERS

WINNER	AWARD	YEAR
Earl Faison	AFL Rookie of the Year	1961
Earl Faison	AFL All-Star Game co-MVP	1963
Keith Lincoln	AFL All-Star Game co-MVP	1964
Keith Lincoln	AFL All-Star Game co-MVP	1965
Frank Buncom	AFL All-Star Game co-MVP	1966
Speedy Duncan	AFL All-Star Game co-MVP	1969
John Hadl	AFL All-Star Game MVP	1970
Don Woods	NFL Offensive Rookie of the Year	1974
Kellen Winslow	Pro Bowl co-MVP	1982
Dan Fouts	Pro Bowl co-MVP	1983
Leslie O'Neal	NFL Defensive Rookie of the Year	1986
Shawne Merriman	NFL Defensive Rookie of the Year	2005
LaDainian Tomlinson	NFL Most Valuable Player	2006

Speedy Duncan

John Hadl

Shawne Merriman

CHARGERS ACHIEVEMENTS

ACHIEVEMENT	YEAR
AFL Western Division Champions	1960
AFL Western Division Champions	1961
AFL Western Division Champions	1963
AFL Champions	1963
AFL Western Division Champions	1964
AFL Western Division Champions	1965
AFC West Champions	1979
AFC West Champions	1980
AFC West Champions	1981
AFC West Champions	1992
AFC West Champions	1994
AFC Champions	1994
AFC West Champions	2004
AFC West Champions	2006
AFC West Champions	2007
AFC West Champions	2008
AFC West Champions	2009

ABOVE: Walt Sweeney and Ernie Wright starred for the 1963 AFL champs. **LEFT**: Norv Turner led San Diego to the 2008 AFC title game.

Pinpoints

The history of a football team is made up of many smaller stories. These stories take place all over the map—not just in the city a team calls "home." Match the pushpins on these maps to the **Team Facts**, and you will begin to see the story of the Chargers unfold!

1 San Diego, California—*The team has played here since 1961.*

2 San Francisco, California—*Dan Fouts was born here.*

3 Seattle, Washington—*Don Coryell was born here.*

4 Minneapolis, Minnesota—*Sid Gillman was born here.*

5 Detroit, Michigan—*Antonio Gates was born here.*

6 Lawrence, Kansas—*John Hadl was born here.*

7 Angleton, Texas—*Quentin Jammer was born here.*

8 Homer, Louisiana—*Paul Lowe was born here.*

9 Miami, Florida—*The Chargers played in Super Bowl XXIX here.*

10 Pittsburgh, Pennsylvania—*The Chargers won the 1994 AFC championship here.*

11 Newport News, Virginia—*Earl Faison was born here.*

12 Tonga—*Alfred Pupunu was born here.*

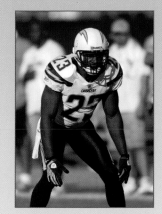

Quentin Jammer

12

Glossary

👤 **AFC CHAMPIONSHIP GAME**—The game played to determine which AFC team will go to the Super Bowl.

👤 **AFC WEST**—A division for teams that play in the western part of the country.

👤 **AFL CHAMPIONSHIP GAME**—The game that decided the winner of the American Football League.

👤 **ALL-AFL**—An honor given to the best players at each position in the AFL.

👤 **ALL-PRO**—An honor given to the best players at their positions at the end of each season.

👤 **AMERICAN FOOTBALL CONFERENCE (AFC)**—One of two groups of teams that make up the NFL.

👤 **AMERICAN FOOTBALL LEAGUE (AFL)**—The football league that began play in 1960 and later merged with the NFL.

🧠 *DECADE*—A period of 10 years; also specific periods, such as the 1950s.

👤 **DRAFT**—The annual meeting during which teams choose from a group of the best college players.

🧠 *DRAMATIC*—Sudden or surprising.

👤 **FIELD GOAL**—A goal from the field, kicked over the crossbar and between the goal posts. A field goal is worth three points.

🧠 *GENERATION*—A period of years roughly equal to the time it takes for a person to be born, grow up, and have children.

👤 **HALL OF FAME**—The museum in Canton, Ohio, where football's greatest players are honored.

👤 **INTERCEPTIONS**—Passes that are caught by the defensive team.

🧠 *LOGO*—A symbol or design that represents a company or team.

🧠 *MEDIEVAL*—From a period of time in Europe associated with the Middle Ages.

👤 **MOST VALUABLE PLAYER (MVP)**—The award given each year to the league's best player; also given to the best player in the Super Bowl and Pro Bowl.

👤 **NATIONAL FOOTBALL LEAGUE (NFL)**—The league that started in 1920 and is still operating today.

👤 **OVERTIME**—The extra period played when a game is tied after 60 minutes.

👤 **PLAYOFFS**—The games played after the regular season to determine which teams play in the Super Bowl.

🧠 *POISE*—Calm and confidence.

👤 **POSTSEASON**—Another term for playoffs.

🧠 *POTENTIAL*—The ability to become better.

👤 **PRO BOWL**—The NFL's all-star game, played after the regular season.

🧠 *PROFESSIONAL*—Paid to play.

👤 **QUARTERBACK RATING**—A statistic that measures how well a quarterback has played.

👤 **SACK**—Tackle the quarterback behind the line of scrimmage.

👤 **SECONDARY**—The part of the defense made up by the cornerbacks and safeties.

👤 **SUPER BOWL**—The championship of the NFL, played between the winners of the National Football Conference and the American Football Conference.

🧠 *UNDERDOGS*—A group of people not expected to achieve a goal or succeed.

🧠 *VETERAN*—A player with great experience.

👤 **WESTERN DIVISION**—A group of teams that play in the western part of the country.

OVERTIME

TEAM SPIRIT introduces a great way to stay up to date with your team! Visit our **OVERTIME** link and get connected to the latest and greatest updates. **OVERTIME** serves as a young reader's ticket to an exclusive web page—with more stories, fun facts, team records, and photos of the Chargers. Content is updated during and after each season. The **OVERTIME** feature also enables readers to send comments and letters to the author!
Log onto:

www.norwoodhousepress.com/library.aspx
and click on the tab: **TEAM SPIRIT** to access **OVERTIME**.

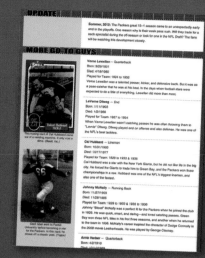

Read all the books in the series to learn more about professional sports. For a complete listing of the baseball, basketball, football, and hockey teams in the **TEAM SPIRIT** series, visit our website at:

www.norwoodhousepress.com/library.aspx

On the Road

SAN DIEGO CHARGERS
9449 Friars Road
San Diego, California 92108
858-874-4500
www.chargers.com

THE PRO FOOTBALL HALL OF FAME
2121 George Halas Drive NW
Canton, Ohio 44708
330-456-8207
www.profootballhof.com

On the Bookshelf

To learn more about the sport of football, look for these books at your library or bookstore:

- Frederick, Shane. *The Best of Everything Football Book.* North Mankato, Minnesota: Capstone Press, 2011.

- Jacobs, Greg. *The Everything Kids' Football Book: The All-Time Greats, Legendary Teams, Today's Superstars—And Tips on Playing Like a Pro.* Avon, Massachusetts: Adams Media Corporation, 2010.

- Editors of *Sports Illustrated for Kids. 1st and 10: Top 10 Lists of Everything in Football.* New York, New York: Sports Illustrated Books, 2011.

Index

PAGE NUMBERS IN **BOLD** REFER TO ILLUSTRATIONS.

About the Author

MARK STEWART has written more than 50 books on football and over 150 sports books for kids. He grew up in New York City during the 1960s rooting for the Giants and Jets, and was lucky enough to meet players from both teams. Mark comes from a family of writers. His grandfather was Sunday Editor of *The New York Times,* and his mother was Articles Editor of *Ladies' Home Journal* and *McCall's.* Mark has profiled hundreds of athletes over the past 25 years. He has also written several books about his native New York and New Jersey, his home today. Mark is a graduate of Duke University, with a degree in history. He lives and works in a home overlooking Sandy Hook, New Jersey. You can contact Mark through the Norwood House Press website.